THE ART OF THE LATHE

Poems by B.H. Fairchild

ALICE JAMES BOOKS
Farmington, Maine

For Locie Marie Fairchild

LIBRARY OF CONGRESS CATALOGING-IN-PUBLICATION DATA
Fourth Printing
Printed in the United States of America

Fairchild, B.H.
The art of the lathe : poems / B.H. Fairchild.
p. cm.
ISBN 1-882295-16-1
1. Lathes—Poetry. I. Title.
PS3556.A3625A89 1998
811'.54—DC 21   97-29398
CIP

Alice James Books gratefully acknowledges support from the University
of Maine at Farmington and the National Endowment for the Arts.

Copyright 1998 by B.H. Fairchild
All rights reserved
Typeset and design by Lisa Clark   Printing by Thomson-Shore

Alice James Books are published by the Alice James Poetry Cooperative, Inc.
University of Maine at Farmington 238 Main Street
Farmington, Maine 04938

The Art of the Lathe

Contents

Introduction by Anthony Hecht / i

Beauty / 11

The Invisible Man / 19

All the People in Hopper's Paintings / 21

The Book of Hours / 24

Cigarettes / 26

Speaking the Names / 28

The Machinist, Teaching His Daughter to Play the Piano / 30

In the House of the Latin Professor / 32

The Himalayas / 34

Body and Soul / 35

Airlifting Horses / 39

Work / 41

Old Men Playing Basketball / 45

Old Women / 47

Song / 48

At the Excavation of Liberal, Kansas / 49

Thermoregulation in Winter Moths / 53

Kansas / 55

Keats / 56

The Ascension of Ira Campbell / 57

The *Dumka* / 58

A Model of Downtown Los Angeles, 1940 / 60

After the Storm / 63

The Children / 65

Little Boy / 67

Two Photographs / 68

The Welder, Visited by the Angel of Mercy / 70

The Death of a Small Town / 72

The Art of the Lathe / 73

Notes / 76

Acknowledgments / 77

Introduction

"When a poet's mind is perfectly equipped for its work, it is constantly amalgamating disparate experience; the ordinary man's experience is chaotic, irregular, fragmentary. The latter falls in love, or reads Spinoza, and these experiences have nothing to do with each other, or with the noise of the typewriter or the smell of cooking; in the mind of the poet these experiences are always forming new wholes." This famous formulation of T.S. Eliot appears in a 1921 essay, ostensibly about the metaphysical poets of the seventeenth century, but in fact at least as descriptive of Eliot's own poetic practice.

Yet however well these words may apply to Donne or Marvell or to Eliot himself, they seem as if they were commissioned to describe the poems of B.H. Fairchild in this wonderful collection, *The Art of the Lathe*. Both the "art" and the "lathe" weave their ways through this book, along with other topics and themes that compel Mr. Fairchild's ductile imagination. His mind seems to work with a sort of limpid smoothness that will allow him (in a poem called "Beauty") to close with a sentence that runs for 36 lines— a long-breathed flowing that seems not only Miltonic but biblical because of the many conjunctive "ands"—but which at the same time is filled with beautiful and unexpected turns that link "the sweat and grease of the day's labor" with Donatello's *David*, the death of Hart Crane, and a machine shop.

Another poem, called "The Book of Hours," begins,

> Like the blue angels of the nativity, the museum patrons
> hover around the art historian, who has arrived frazzled
> and limp after waking late in her boyfriend's apartment.

The worshipful posture of the museum-goers, the implied identification of the art historian with the Virgin Mary, around whom the angels of the nativity cluster, the consequent pungency of the erotic note of the former's belated arrival from a boyfriend's apartment begin a wonderful blending of elements that include the miniaturist Limbourg brothers and a Book of Hours (probably the *Tres Riches Heures* of the Duc de Berry) for which they provided the celebrated illuminations, and the all-but-forgotten and anonymous scribal monks who, in their ascetic isolation, copied the texts of this vellum-paged book of private devotions.

The imaginative braiding and infibulation of the disjunctive regions of the mind and experience occurs not only within the confines of individual poems but as an eloquent feature of the contrapuntal design of the entire book. With elegance and restrained subtlety, Mr. Fairchild interweaves topics that become something like musical themes in his work: 1) men at play, chiefly baseball and basketball, 2) the desolation of certain mid-western small towns, 3) parents and their children; ageing and memory, 4) music itself, and many forms of art, 5) work of a highly specialized and demanding kind, chiefly machine-shop work.

But none of these ever appears in isolation from one or several of the others, so that in "The Ascension of Ira Campbell," concerning a man on an oil rig, the poet is able to join "five thousand feet of drill pipe" with Wittgenstein's *Tractatus*, and the first line of a poem titled "Keats" goes, "I knew him. He ran the lathe next to mine." Such details, as well as much else in the book, should remind us that Mr. Fairchild knows at first hand about industrial precision instruments and the sort of specialized labor that entails bodily exhaustion, exacting discipline, and physical danger. This makes of him an altogether different breed of poet from, say, Byron, Tennyson, Cummings, Shelley, Pound, Browning and Yeats, all of whom, by fate or fortune, were never obliged to work for a living. In Mr. Fairchild's generous and ample mind, these industrial skills relate both to despairing fatigue and to the exactions and exactitudes of art. The poems modulate between tones of reverence, grave tenderness, and courageous resignation. They also include what is certainly the best baseball poem I know: "Body and Soul."

Each reader will make his or her own list of favorites, and I want to volunteer my own: "Beauty," "All the People in Hopper's Paintings," "The Book of Hours," "Speaking the Names," "Body and Soul," "Old Men Playing Basketball," "Old Women," "Keats," "The Ascension of Ira Campbell," "A Model of Downtown Los Angeles, 1940," "The Children," "The Welder, Visited by the Angel of Mercy," and "The Art of the Lathe." Anyone who can lay claim to the authorship of that much excellent poetry wins my unqualified and grateful admiration.

Anthony Hecht

How hard these people played, and how they struggled to do well, and how well they did, and what a profound isolation it was to long for beauty and grace in the industrial heartland of the United States.

E.L. Doctorow, attending a local symphony concert with James Wright in Wheeling, West Virginia

Beauty

Therefore,
Their sons grow suicidally beautiful . . .
  —James Wright, "Autumn Begins in Martin's Ferry, Ohio"

I.
We are at the Bargello in Florence, and she says,
what are you thinking? and I say, *beauty*, thinking
of how very far we are now from the machine shop
and the dry fields of Kansas, the treeless horizons
of slate skies and the muted passions of roughnecks
and scrabble farmers drunk and romantic enough
to weep more or less silently at the darkened end
of the bar out of, what else, loneliness, meaning
the ache of thwarted desire, of, in a word, *beauty*,
or rather its absence, and it occurs to me again
that no male member of my family has ever used
this word in my hearing or anyone else's except
in reference, perhaps, to a new pickup or dead deer.
This insight, this backward vision, first came to me
as a young man as some weirdness of the air waves
slipped through the static of our new Motorola
with a discussion of *beauty* between Robert Penn Warren
and Paul Weiss at Yale College. We were in Kansas
eating barbecue-flavored potato chips and waiting
for *Father Knows Best* to float up through the snow
of rural TV in 1963. I felt transported, stunned.
Here were two grown men discussing "beauty"
seriously and with dignity as if they and the topic
were as normal as normal topics of discussion
between men such as soybean prices or why
the commodities market was a sucker's game
or Oklahoma football or Gimpy Neiderland

11

almost dying from his hemorrhoid operation.
They were discussing beauty and tossing around
allusions to Plato and Aristotle and someone
named Pater, and they might be homosexuals.
That would be a natural conclusion, of course,
since here were two grown men talking about "beauty"
instead of scratching their crotches and cursing
the goddamned government trying to run everybody's
business. Not a beautiful thing, that. The government.
Not beautiful, though a man would not use that word.
One time my Uncle Ross from California called my mom's
Sunday dinner centerpiece "lovely," and my father
left the room, clearly troubled by the word "lovely"
coupled probably with the very idea of California
and the fact that my Uncle Ross liked to tap-dance.
The light from the venetian blinds, the autumn,
silver Kansas light laving the table that Sunday,
is what I recall now because it was beautiful,
though I of course would not have said so then, *beautiful*,
as so many moments forgotten but later remembered
come back to us in slants and pools and uprisings of light,
beautiful in itself, but more beautiful mingled
with memory, the light leaning across my mother's
carefully set table, across the empty chair
beside my Uncle Ross, the light filtering down
from the green plastic slats in the roof of the machine shop
where I worked with my father so many afternoons,
standing or crouched in pools of light and sweat with men
who knew the true meaning of labor and money and other
hard, true things and did not, did not ever, use the word, *beauty*.

II.

Late November, shadows gather in the shop's north end,
and I'm watching Bobby Sudduth do piece work on the Hobbs.
He fouls another cut, *motherfucker, fucking bitch machine,*
and starts over, sloppy, slow, about two joints away
from being fired, but he just doesn't give a shit.
He sets the bit again, white wrists flashing in the lamplight
and showing botched, blurred tattoos, both from a night
in Tijuana, and continues his sexual autobiography,
that's right, fucked my own sister, and I'll tell you, bud,
it wasn't bad. Later, in the Philippines, the clap:
as far as I'm concerned, any man who hasn't had V.D.
just isn't a man. I walk away, knowing I have just heard
the dumbest remark ever uttered by man or animal.
The air around me hums in a dark metallic bass,
light spilling like grails of milk as someone opens
the mammoth shop door. A shrill, sullen truculence
blows in like dust devils, the hot wind nagging
my blousy overalls, and in the sideyard the winch truck
backfires and stalls. The sky yellows. Barn sparrows cry
in the rafters. That afternoon in Dallas Kennedy is shot.

Two weeks later sitting around on rotary tables
and traveling blocks whose bearings litter the shop floor
like huge eggs, we close our lunch boxes and lean back
with cigarettes and watch smoke and dust motes rise and drift
into sunlight. All of us have seen the newscasts,
photographs from *Life*, have sat there in our cavernous rooms,
assassinations and crowds flickering over our faces,
some of us have even dreamed it, sleeping through
the TV's drone and flutter, seen her arm reaching

13

across the lank body, black suits rushing in like moths,
and the long snake of the motorcade come to rest,
then the announcer's voice as we wake astonished in the dark.
We think of it now, staring at the tin ceiling like a giant screen,
what a strange goddamned country, as Bobby Sudduth
arches a wadded Fritos bag at the time clock and says,
Oswald, from that far, you got to admit, that shot was a beauty.

III.
The following summer. A black Corvette gleams like a slice
of onyx in the sideyard, driven there by two young men
who look like Marlon Brando and mention Hollywood
when Bobby asks where they're from. The foreman, my father,
has hired them because we're backed up with work, both shop
and yard strewn with rig parts, flat-bed haulers rumbling
in each day lugging damaged drawworks, and we are desperate.
The noise is awful, a gang of roughnecks from a rig
on down-time shouting orders, our floor hands knee-deep
in the drawwork's gears heating the frozen sleeves and bushings
with cutting torches until they can be hammered loose.
The iron shell bangs back like a drum-head. Looking
for some peace, I walk onto the pipe rack for a quick smoke,
and this is the way it begins for me, this memory,
this strangest of all memories of the shop and the men
who worked there, because the silence has come upon me
like the shadow of cranes flying overhead as they would
each autumn, like the quiet and imperceptible turning
of a season, the shop has grown suddenly still here
in the middle of the workday, and I turn to look
through the tall doors where the machinists stand now

14

with their backs to me, the lathes whining down together,
and in the shop's center I see them standing in a square
of light, the two men from California, as the welders
lift their black masks, looking up, and I see their faces first,
the expressions of children at a zoo, perhaps,
or after a first snow, as the two men stand naked,
their clothes in little piles on the floor as if they
are about to go swimming, and I recall how fragile
and pale their bodies seemed against the iron and steel
of the drill presses and milling machines and lathes.
I did not know the word, *exhibitionist*, then, and so
for a moment it seemed only a problem of memory,
that they had *forgotten* somehow where they were,
that this was not the locker room after the game,
that they were not taking a shower, that this was not
the appropriate place, and they would then remember,
and suddenly embarrassed, begin shyly to dress again.
But they did not, and in memory they stand frozen
and poised as two models in a drawing class,
of whom the finished sketch might be said, though not by me
nor any man I knew, to be beautiful, they stand there
forever, with the time clock ticking behind them,
time running on but not moving, like the white tunnel
of silence between the snap of the ball and the thunderclap
of shoulder pads that never seems to come and then
there it is, and I hear a quick intake of breath
on my right behind the Hobbs and it is Bobby Sudduth
with what I think now was not just anger but a kind
of terror on his face, an animal wildness
in the eyes and the jaw tight, making ropes in his neck
while in a long blur with his left hand raised and gripping

an iron file he is moving toward the men who wait
attentive and motionless as deer trembling in a clearing,
and instantly there is my father between Bobby
and the men as if he were waking them after a long sleep,
reaching out to touch the shoulder of the blonde one
as he says in a voice almost terrible in its gentleness,
its discretion, *you boys will have to leave now.*
He takes one look at Bobby who is shrinking back
into the shadows of the Hobbs, then walks quickly back
to his office at the front of the shop, and soon
the black Corvette with the orange California plates
is squealing onto Highway 54 heading west into the sun.

IV.

So there they are, as I will always remember them,
the men who were once fullbacks or tackles or guards
in their three-point stances knuckling into the mud,
hungry for highschool glory and the pride of their fathers,
eager *to gallop terribly against each other's bodies,*
each man in his body looking out now at the nakedness
of a body like his, men who each autumn had followed
their fathers into the pheasant-rich fields of Kansas
and as boys had climbed down from the Allis-Chalmers
after plowing their first straight furrow, licking the dirt
from their lips, the hand of the father resting lightly
upon their shoulder, men who in the oven-warm winter
kitchens of Baptist households saw after a bath the body
of the father and felt diminished by it, who that same
winter in the abandoned schoolyard felt the odd intimacy
of their fist against the larger boy's cheekbone
but kept hitting, ferociously, and walked away

feeling for the first time the strength, the *abundance,*
of their own bodies. And I imagine the men
that evening after the strangest day of their lives,
after they have left the shop without speaking
and made the long drive home alone in their pickups,
I see them in their little white frame houses on the edge
of town adrift in the long silence of the evening turning
finally to their wives, touching without speaking the hair
which she has learned to let fall about her shoulders
at this hour of night, lifting the white nightgown
from her body as she in turn unbuttons his work shirt
heavy with the sweat and grease of the day's labor until
they stand naked before each other and begin to touch
in a slow choreography of familiar gestures their bodies,
she touching his chest, his hand brushing her breasts,
and he does not say the word "beautiful" because
he cannot and never has, and she does not say it
because it would embarrass him or any other man
she has ever known, though it is precisely the word
I am thinking now as I stand before Donatello's David
with my wife touching my sleeve, *what are you thinking?*
and I think of the letter from my father years ago
describing the death of Bobby Sudduth, a single shot
from a twelve-gauge which he held against his chest,
the death of the heart, I suppose, *a kind of terrible beauty,*
as someone said of the death of Hart Crane, though that is
surely a perverse use of the word, and I was stunned then,
thinking of the damage men will visit upon their bodies,
what are you thinking? she asks again, and so I begin
to tell her about a strange afternoon in Kansas,
about something I have never spoken of, and we walk
to a window where the shifting light spreads a sheen

along the casement, and looking out, we see the city
blazing like miles of uncut wheat, the farthest buildings
taken in their turn, and the great dome, the way
the metal roof of the machine shop, I tell her,
would break into flame late on an autumn day, with such beauty.

The Invisible Man

We are kids with orange Jujubes stuck to our chins
and licorice sticks snaking out of our jeans pockets,
and we see him, or rather don't see him, when the bandages
uncoil from his face and lo, there's nothing between
the hat and suit. It is wonderful, this pure nothing,
but we begin to be troubled by the paradoxes of non-existence
(Can he pee? If he itches, can he scratch? If he eats
Milk Duds, do they disappear?). Sure, standing around
in the girls' lockerroom unobserved or floating erasers
in math class, who could resist, but the enigma
of sheer absence, the loss of the body, of *who we are*,
continues to grind against us even into the Roy Rogers
western that follows. The pungent Vista Vision embodiments
of good and evil—this clear-eyed young man with watermelon
voice and high principles, the fat, unshaven dipshits
with no respect for old ladies or hard-working Baptist
farmers—none of this feels quite solid anymore. Granted,
it's the world as the world appears, but *provisional* somehow,
a shadow, a ghost, dragging behind every rustled cow
or runaway stagecoach, and though afterwards the cloud
of insubstantiality lifts and fades as we stroll out
grimacing into the hard sunlight, there is that
slight tremble of deja-vu years later in Philosophy 412
as Professor Caws mumbles on about essence and existence,
being and nothingness, and *Happy Trails to You* echoes
from the far end of the hall.
                              In *The Invisible Man*
sometimes we could see the thread or thin wire that lifted
the gun from the thief's hand, and at the Hearst mansion
only days ago a sign explained that the orchestra
of Leonard Slye entertained the zillionaire and his Hollywood
friends on spring evenings caressed by ocean breezes

and the scent of gardenias. You can almost see them swaying
to *Mood Indigo* or *Cherokee*, champagne glasses in hand:
Chaplin, Gable, Marion Davies, Herman Mankiewicz,
and cruising large as the Titanic, William Randolph Hearst,
Citizen Kane himself. Leonard Slye sees this, too, along with
the Roman statuary and rare medieval tapestries, and thinks,
someday, someday, and becomes invisible so that he
can appear later as Roy Rogers and make movies in
Victorville, California, where Mankiewicz and Orson Welles
will write the story of an enormous man who misplaced
his childhood and tried to call it back on his death-bed.
O Leonard Slye, lifting Roy's six-gun from its holster,
O Hearst, dreaming of Rosebud and raping the castles of Europe,
O America, with your dreams of money and power,
small boys sit before your movie screens invisible
to themselves, waiting for the next episode, in which they
stumble blind into daylight and the body of the world.

All the People in Hopper's Paintings

All the people in Hopper's paintings walk by me
here in the twilight the way our neighbors
would stroll by of an evening in my hometown
smiling and waving as I leaned against
the front-porch railing and hated them all
and the place I had grown up in. I smoked
my Pall Mall with a beautifully controlled rage
in the manner of James Dean and imagined
life beyond the plains in the towns of Hopper
where people were touched by the light of the real.

The people in Hopper's paintings were lonely
as I was and lived in brown rooms whose
long, sad windows looked out on the roofs
of brown buildings in the towns that made
them lonely. Or they lived in coffee shops
and cafes at three a.m. under decadent flowers
of cigarette smoke as I thought I would have
if there had been such late-night conspiracy
in the town that held me but offered nothing.
And now they gather around with their bland,

mysterious faces in half-shadow, many still
bearing the hard plane of light that found them
from the left side of the room, as in Vermeer,
others wearing the dark splotches of early
evening across their foreheads and chins that said
they were, like me, tragic, dark, undiscovered:
the manicurist from the barber shop buried
beneath a pyramid of light and a clock frozen
at eleven, the woman sitting on the bed
too exhausted with the hopelessness of brick walls

and barber poles and Rhinegold ads to dress
herself in street clothes. The wordless, stale
affair with the filling station attendant
was the anteroom to heartbreak. The gloom
of his stupid uniform and black tie beneath
the three white bulbs blinking MOBILGAS into
the woods that loomed bleak as tombstones
on the edge of town; the drab backroom
with its Prestone cans and sighing Vargas girls
and grease rags; his panting, pathetic *loneliness*.

But along the white island of the station,
the luminous squares from its windows
lying quietly like carpets on the pavement
had been my hope, my sense then of the real world
beyond the familiar one, like the blazing cafe
of the nighthawks casting the town into shadow,
or the beach house of the sea watchers
who sat suspended on a verandah of light,
stunned by the flat, hard sea of the real.
Everywhere was that phosphorescence, that pale

wash of promise lifting roofs and chimneys
out of dullness, out of the ordinary that I
could smell in my workclothes coming home
from a machine shop lined with men who stood
at lathes and looked out of windows and wore
the same late-afternoon layers of sunlight
that Hopper's people carried to hotel rooms
and cafeterias. Why was their monotony
blessed, their melancholy apocalyptic, while
my days hung like red rags from my pockets

as I stood, welding torch in hand, and searched
the horizon with the eyes and straight mouth
of Hopper's women? If they had come walking
toward me, those angels of boredom, if they
had arrived clothed in their robes of light,
would I have recognized them? If all those women
staring out of windows had risen from their desks
and unmade beds, and the men from their offices
and sun-draped brownstones, would I have known?
Would I have felt their light hands touching

my face the way infants do when people
seem no more real than dreams or picture books?
The girl in the blue gown leaning from her door
at high noon, the gray-haired gentleman
in the hotel by the railroad, holding his cigarette
so delicately, they have found me, and we
walk slowly through the small Kansas town
that held me and offered nothing, where the light
fell through the windows of brown rooms, and people
looked out, strangely, as if they had been painted there.

The Book of Hours

Like the blue angels of the nativity, the museum patrons
hover around the art historian, who has arrived frazzled
and limp after waking late in her boyfriend's apartment.
And here, she notes, *the Procession of St. Gregory,*
where atop Hadrian's mausoleum the angel of death
returns his bloody sword to its scabbard, and staring
down at the marble floor, liquid in the slanted
silver light of mid-morning, she ponders briefly
the polished faces of her audience: seraphim gazing
heavenward at the golden throne, or, as she raises
her tired eyes to meet their eyes, the evolving souls
of purgatory, bored as the inhabitants of some
fashionable European spa sunbathing on boulders.
And here, notice the lovely treatment of St. John
on Patmos, robed in blue and gold, and she tells the story
of gall-nuts, goats' skins dried and stretched into vellum—
the word *vellum* delicious in its saying, caressed
in her mouth like a fat breakfast plum—lapis lazuli
crushed into pools of ultramarine blue, and gold foil
hammered thin enough to float upon the least breath,
the scribes hastily scraping gold flakes into ceramic cups,
curling their toes against the cold like her lover stepping
out of bed in that odd, delicate way of his, wisps of gold
drifting like miniature angels onto the scriptorium's
stone floor, and dogs' teeth to polish the gold leaf
as transcendent in its beauty, she says, *as the medieval*
mind conceived the soul to be.

The patrons are beginning
to wander now as she points to the crucifixion scene,
done to perfection by the Limbourg brothers, the skull and bones
of Adam lying scattered beneath the Roman soldier's horse,

and the old custodian wipes palm prints from the glass, the monks
breathe upon their fingertips and pray against the hard winter,
and the art historian recalls the narrow shafts of light tapping
the breakfast table, the long curve of his back in half-shadow,
the bed's rumpled sheets lifted by an ocean breeze
as if they were the weightless gold leaf of the spirit.

Cigarettes

Gross, loathsome. Trays and plates loaded
like rain gutters, butts crumpled and damp with gin,
ashes still shedding the rank breath of exhaustion—
nevertheless, an integral part of human evolution,
like reading. Cigarettes possess the nostalgic potency
of old songs: hand on the steering wheel, fat pack
of Pall Malls snug under my sleeve, skinny bicep
pressed against the car door so my muscle bulges,
and my girl, wanting a smoke, touches my arm.
Or 3 a.m. struggling with the Chekhov paper, I break
the blue stamp with my thumb, nudge open petals of foil,
and the bloom of nicotine puts me right back in the feedstore
where my grandfather used to trade—leather, oats, burlap,
and red sawdust. Or at the beach, minute flares floating
in the deep dark, rising, falling in the hands of aunts
and uncles telling the old stories, drowsy with beer,
waves lapping the sand and dragging their voices down.
Consider the poverty of lungs drawing ordinary air,
the unreality of it, the lie it tells about quotidian existence.
Bad news craves cigarettes, whole heaps of them, sucking
in the bad air the way the drowning gulp river water,
though in hospital rooms I've seen grief let smoke
gather slowly into pools that rise, and rise again
to nothing. I've studied the insincere purity
of a mouth without the cigarette that gives the air form,
the hand focus, the lips a sense of identity.
The way Shirley Levin chattered after concerts:
her fingers mimicking piano keys and the cigarette
they held galloping in heart-like fibrillations until
the thrill of it had unravelled in frayed strands of smoke.
1979: *Sweet Lorraine*, seventh, eighth chorus, and

I'm looking at the small black scallops above the keyboard,
a little history of smoke and jazz, improvisation as
a kind of forgetting. The music of cigarettes:
dawn stirs and lifts the smoke in dove-gray striations
that hang, then break, scatter, and regroup along
the sill where paperbacks warp in sunlight and the cat
claws housespiders. Cigarettes are the only way
to make bleakness nutritional, or at least useful,
something to do while feeling terrified. They cling
to the despair of certain domestic scenes—my father,
for instance, smoking L&M's all night in the kitchen,
a sea of smoke risen to neck-level as I wander in
like some small craft drifting and lost in fog
while a distant lighthouse flares awhile and swings away.
Yes, they kill you, but so do television and bureaucrats
and the drugged tedium of certain rooms piped
with tasteful music where we have all sat waiting
for someone to enter with a silver plate laden
with Camels and Lucky Strikes, someone who leans
into our ears and tells us that the day's work is done,
and done well, offers us black coffee in white cups,
and whispers the way trees whisper, *yes, yes, oh yes.*

Speaking the Names

When frost first enters the air
in the country of moon and stars,
the world has glass edges, and the hard glint
of crystals seeping over iron
makes even the abandoned tractor seem all night sky and starlight.

On the backporch taking deep breaths like some miracle cure,
breathe, let the spirit move you,
here I am after the long line of cigarettes
that follows grief like a curse, trying to breathe, revive,
in this land of revivals and lost farms . . .

It is no good to grow up hating the rich.
In spring I would lie down among pale anemone and primrose
and listen to the river's darkening hymn, and soon
the clouds were unravelling like the frayed sleeves of field hands,
and ideology had flown with the sparrows.

The cottonwood that sheltered the hen house is a stump now,
and the hackberries on the north were leveled years ago.
Bluestem hides the cellar, with its sweet gloom of clay walls and
    bottles.
The silo looms over the barn, whose huge door swallowed
    daylight,
where a child could enter his own death.

What became of the boy with nine fingers?
The midwife from Yellow Horse who raised geese?
They turned their backs on the hard life,
and from the tree line along the river they seem to rise now,
her plain dress bronze in moonlight, his wheatshock hair in flames.

Behind me is a house without people. And so, for my sake
I bring them back, watching the quick cloud of vapor that blo
and vanishes with each syllable: *O.T.* and *Nellie Swearingen,*
their children, *Locie, Dorrel, Deanie, Bill,* and the late *Vinna A(*
whose name I speak into the bright and final air.

The Machinist, Teaching His Daughter to Play the Piano

The brown wrist and hand with its raw knuckles and blue nails
        packed with dirt and oil, pause in mid-air,
the fingers arched delicately,

and she mimics him, hand held just so, the wrist loose,
        then swooping down to the wrong chord.
She lifts her hand and tries again.

Drill collars rumble, hammering the nubbin-posts.
        The helper lifts one, turning it slowly,
then lugs it into the lathe's chuck.

The bit shears the dull iron into new metal, falling
        into the steady chant of lathe work,
and the machinist lights a cigarette, holding

in his upturned palms the polonaise he learned at ten,
        then later the easiest waltzes,
etudes, impossible counterpoint

like the voice of his daughter he overhears one night
        standing in the backyard. She is speaking
to herself but not herself, as in prayer,

the listener is some version of herself,
        and the names are pronounced carefully,
self-consciously: Chopin, Mozart,

Scarlatti, . . . these gestures of voice and hands
        suspended over the keyboard
that move like the lathe in its turning

toward music, the wind dragging the hoist chain, the ring
        of iron on iron in the holding rack.
His daughter speaks to him one night,

but not to him, rather someone created between them,
        a listener, there and not there,
a master of lathes, a student of music.

In the House of the Latin Professor

All things fall away: store fronts on the west,
ANGEL'S DELICATESSEN, windows boarded
and laced in day-glow, BLUE KNIGHT AUTO REPAIR
to the north with its verandah of rusted mufflers

and hubcaps of extinct Studebakers.
The diminishing neighborhood sprawls
under dusty folds of sycamore and fading elm,
the high birdhouse out back starling-haunted.

Inside the cottage a bay window translates
the language of sunlight, flaring like baroque
trumpets on the red carpet, shadow-dappled
as the house turns slowly beneath the drift

of tree branch and sun. We have come
to shroud the couch in plastic, spread sheets
over the fat reading chair and the piano's
mahogany gloom, the impossible etude's

blur of black notes. Among a turmoil
of ungraded papers lies the Loeb Classics *Aeneid*
open to the last lesson. Later in the bedroom
we imagine a flourish of light, her husband

loosening the sash of her white silk robe,
his beard brushing the back of her neck.
Amores, the art of love, of words lifting
like vapors on a cold day, the dense vowels

of Ovid and Virgil almost vanished, almost
risen to music. We lock the heavy door
and walk away from the silence, the lone
hexameters of Dido pulsing in an empty house.

The Himalayas

The stewardess' dream of the Himalayas
followed her everywhere: from Omaha
to Baltimore and back, and then to Seattle
and up and down the California coast until
she imagined herself strapped to the wing
just across from seat 7A muttering
little homemade mantras and shivering
in the cold, stiff wind of the inexpressible.
It could hardly go on like this, she thought,
the unending prayer to nothing in particular
whirling around in her head while she held
the yellow mask over her face and demonstrated
correct breathing techniques: the point was
to breathe calmly like angels observing
the final separation of light from a dead star,
or the monk described in the travel book
trying to untangle his legs and stand once more
at the mouth of his cave. The stewardess
delighted in her symmetrical gestures, the dance
of her hands describing the emergency exits
and the overhead lights that made exquisite
small cones in the night for readers and children
afraid of the dark. As the passengers fell asleep
around her, the stewardess reached up to adjust
the overhead whose cone of light rose over her
like some miniature white peak of the Himalayas
as if she were a cave in the Himalayas,
the cave of her own body, perhaps, in which
she sat patiently now, looking out, waiting.

Body and Soul

Half-numb, guzzling bourbon and Coke from coffee mugs,
our fathers fall in love with their own stories, nuzzling
the facts but mauling the truth, and my friend's father begins
to lay out with the slow ease of a blues ballad a story
about sandlot baseball in Commerce, Oklahoma decades ago.
These were men's teams, grown men, some in their thirties
and forties who worked together in zinc mines or on oil rigs,
sweat and khaki and long beers after work, steel guitar music
whanging in their ears, little white rent houses to return to
where their wives complained about money and broken Kenmores
and then said the hell with it and sang *Body and Soul*
in the bathtub and later that evening with the kids asleep
lay in bed stroking their husband's wrist tattoo and smoking
Chesterfields from a fresh pack until everything was O.K.
Well, you get the idea. Life goes on, the next day is Sunday,
another ball game, and the other team shows up one man short.

They say, we're one man short, but can we use this boy,
he's only fifteen years old, and at least he'll make a game.
They take a look at the kid, muscular and kind of knowing
the way he holds his glove, with the shoulders loose,
the thick neck, but then with that boy's face under
a clump of angelic blonde hair, and say, oh, hell, sure,
let's play ball. So it all begins, the men loosening up,
joking about the fat catcher's sex life, it's so bad
last night he had to hump his wife, that sort of thing,
pairing off into little games of catch that heat up into
throwing matches, the smack of the fungo bat, lazy jogging
into right field, big smiles and arcs of tobacco juice,
and the talk that gives a cool, easy feeling to the air,
talk among men normally silent, normally brittle and a little
angry with the empty promise of their lives. But they chatter

and say rock and fire, babe, easy out, and go right ahead
and pitch to the boy, but nothing fancy, just hard fastballs
right around the belt, and the kid takes the first two
but on the third pops the bat around so quick and sure
that they pause a moment before turning around to watch
the ball still rising and finally dropping far beyond
the abandoned tractor that marks left field. Holy shit.
They're pretty quiet watching him round the bases,
but then, what the hell, the kid knows how to hit a ball,
so what, let's play some goddamned baseball here.
And so it goes. The next time up, the boy gets a look
at a very nifty low curve, then a slider, and the next one
is the curve again, and he sends it over the Allis Chalmers,
high and big and sweet. The left fielder just stands there, frozen.
As if this isn't enough, the next time up he bats left-handed.
They can't believe it, and the pitcher, a tall, mean-faced
man from Okarche who just doesn't give a shit anyway
because his wife ran off two years ago leaving him with
three little ones and a rusted-out Dodge with a cracked block,
leans in hard, looking at the fat catcher like he was the sonofabitch
who ran off with his wife, leans in and throws something
out of the dark, green hell of forbidden fastballs, something
that comes in at the knees and then leaps viciously towards
the kid's elbow. He swings exactly the way he did right-handed,
and they all turn like a chorus line toward deep right field
where the ball loses itself in sagebrush and the sad burnt
dust of dustbowl Oklahoma. It is something to see.

But why make a long story long: runs pile up on both sides,
the boy comes around five times, and five times the pitcher
is cursing both God and His mother as his chew of tobacco sours
into something resembling horse piss, and a ragged and bruised

Spalding baseball disappears into the far horizon. Goodnight,
Irene. They have lost the game and some painful side bets
and they have been suckered. And it means nothing to them
though it should to you when they are told the boy's name is
Mickey Mantle. And that's the story, and those are the facts.
But the facts are not the truth. I think, though, as I scan
the faces of these old men now lost in the innings of their youth,
I think I know what the truth of this story is, and I imagine
it lying there in the weeds behind that Allis Chalmers
just waiting for the obvious question to be asked: why, oh
why in hell didn't they just throw around the kid, walk him,
after he hit the third homer? Anybody would have,
especially nine men with disappointed wives and dirty socks
and diminishing expectations for whom winning at anything
meant everything. Men who knew how to play the game,
who had talent when the other team had nothing except this ringer
who without a pitch to hit was meaningless, and they could
    go home
with their little two-dollar side bets and stride into the house
singing *If You've Got the Money, Honey, I've Got the Time*
with a bottle of Southern Comfort under their arms and grab
Dixie or May Ella up and dance across the gray linoleum
as if it were V-Day all over again. But they did not.
And they did not because they were men, and this was a boy.
And they did not because sometimes after making love,
after smoking their Chesterfields in the cool silence and
listening to the big bands on the radio that sounded so glamorous,
so distant, they glanced over at their wives and noticed the lines
growing heavier around the eyes and mouth, felt what their wives
felt: that Les Brown and Glenn Miller and all those dancing
    couples
and in fact all possibility of human gaiety and light-heartedness

37

were as far away and unreachable as Times Square or the Avalon
ballroom. They did not because of the gray linoleum lying there
in the half-dark, the free calendar from the local mortuary
that said one day was pretty much like another, the work gloves
looped over the doorknob like dead squirrels. And they did not
because they had gone through a depression and a war that
    had left
them with the idea that being a man in the eyes of their fathers
and everyone else had cost them just too goddamned much to lay it
at the feet of a fifteen year-old boy. And so they did not walk him,
and lost, but at least had some ragged remnant of themselves
to take back home. But there is one thing more, though it is not
a fact. When I see my friend's father staring hard into the
    bottomless
well of home plate as Mantle's fifth homer heads toward Arkansas,
I know that this man with the half-orphaned children and
worthless Dodge has also encountered for his first and possibly
only time the vast gap between talent and genius, has seen
as few have in the harsh light of an Oklahoma Sunday, the blonde
and blue-eyed bringer of truth, who will not easily be forgiven.

Airlifting Horses

Boy soldiers gawk and babble, eyes rapt
in what seems like worship as the horses rise
in the bludgeoned air. A brush fire is swarming
roads and highways, and the last way out is up

or a flatboat in the lagoon. We used to drop
the reins and let them race there, hurdling
driftwood, heaps of kelp, waves lapping the sand
in a lace maker's weave of sea and foam.

Now they're startled into flight, and the air,
stunned and savaged by the propeller's flail,
beats us back. Its sudden thunder must be a storm
their skins have for the first time failed to sense.

Cowering beneath the blades, we have cradled them
like babies, strapped them in slings strong enough
to lug trucks, and their silence is the purest tone
of panic. Their great necks crane and arch,

the eyes flame, and their spidery shadows,
big-bellied and stiff-legged, swallow us,
then dwindle to blotches on the tarmac
as they lift. The cable that hauls them up

like some kind of spiritual harness vanishes
from sight. Their hooves pummel the heavy wind,
and the earth they rode a thousand days or more
falls away in hunks of brown and yellow.

Even the weight of their bodies has abandoned them,
but now they are the gods we always wanted:
winged as any myth, strange, distant, real,
and we will never be ourselves till they return.

Work

Work is a transient form of mechanical energy by means
of which certain transformations of other forms of energy
are brought about through the agency of a force acting through
a distance. . . . Work done by lifting a body stores mechanical
potential energy in the system consisting of the body and the earth.
Work done on a body to set it in motion stores mechanical kinetic
energy in the system of which the body is one part.
       —Handbook of Engineering Fundamentals

I. Work

Drill collars lie on racks and howl
in the blunt wind. A winch truck waits
in the shop yard beside an iron block,
hook and cable coiling down, dragging
through dirt that blows in yellow gusts.

East across a field where the slag sky
of morning bends down, a man walks away
from a white frame house and a woman
who shouts and waves from the back porch.
He can hear the shop doors banging open.

Inside, where the gray light lifts dust
in swirls, tools rest like bodies dull
with sleep, lead-heavy. The lathe
starts its dark groan, the chuck's jaw
gripping an iron round, the bit set.

Outside, the man approaches the iron block,
a rotary table, judging its weight,
the jerk and pull on the hoist chain.
A bad sun heaves the shadow of his house
outward. He bends down. A day begins.

II. The Body

Looping the chain through the block's eyes,
he makes a knot and pulls the cable hook through.
The winch motor starts up, reeling in cable slowly

until it tightens, then drops to a lower gear
and begins to lift. The motor's whine brings
machinists to the shop windows, sends sparrows

fluttering from high-wires where the plains wind
gives its thin moan and sigh. When the brake
is thrown, the block jerks and sways five feet

above the earth, straining to return, popping
a loose cable thread and making the gin poles
screech in their sockets like grief-stricken women.

From the house the man is lost in the blaze of a sun
gorged to bursting and mirrored in the shop's
tin side. The block hangs, black in the red air.

III. The Body and the Earth

Beneath the rotary table the man reaches up
to remove the huge bearings, and oil winds
down his arm like a black rope. He places
each bearing big as a pendulum in the sun

42

where it shines, swathed in grease.
It is the heart of the day, and he feels
the long breeze cool his face and forearms,
wet now with the good sweat of hard work.

The wind scrapes through stubble, making
a papery sound that reminds him of harvest:
him, his father, the field hands crowded around
a beer keg to celebrate the week's cut, dirt

drying to mud on their damp faces, leaving
bruises and black masks. Now, kneeling
in the block's cool shadow, he watches clods
soak up the brown pools of oil and sweat.

IV. The System of Which the Body Is One Part

On the down side of the work day,
when the wind shifts and heat stuns the ground
like an iron brand, the machinists lean
into the shadow of the shop's eaves
and gulp ice water, watching the yard hand now

as he struggles in his black square
to slip each bearing back in place, each steel ball
that mirrors back his eyes, the stubble field, the shop,
the white frame house, the sun, and everything beyond,
the whole circumference of seen and unseen, the world

stretching away in its one last moment when the chain
makes that odd grunting noise, and sighs *click*, and then *click*,
and sings through the eyes of the block as it slams the ground
and the earth takes the thud and the men freeze
and the woman strolls out to see what has happened now
in the system of which the body is one part.

Old Men Playing Basketball

The heavy bodies lunge, the broken language
of fake and drive, glamorous jump shot
slowed to a stutter. Their gestures, in love
again with the pure geometry of curves,

rise toward the ball, falter, and fall away.
On the boards their hands and fingertips
tremble in tense little prayers of reach
and balance. Then, the grind of bone

and socket, the caught breath, the sigh,
the grunt of the body laboring to give
birth to itself. In their toiling and grand
sweeps, I wonder, do they still make love

to their wives, kissing the undersides
of their wrists, dancing the old soft-shoe
of desire? And on the long walk home
from the VFW, do they still sing

to the drunken moon? Stands full, clock
moving, the one in army fatigues
and houseshoes says to himself, *pick and roll*,
and the phrase sounds musical as ever,

radio crooning songs of love after the game,
the girl leaning back in the Chevy's front seat
as her raven hair flames in the shuddering
light of the outdoor movie, and now he drives,

gliding toward the net. A glass wand
of autumn light breaks over the backboard.
Boys rise up in old men, wings begin to sprout
at their backs. The ball turns in the darkening air.

Old Women

They of the trembling hands and liver spots
like a map of Asia, far pale countries of the flesh
wandering as their hands wandered beside me
over texts of Ezekiel and Jeremiah to prophesy
the blues and yellows of next summer's swallowtails
any Sunday morning in the First Methodist Church
of Liberal, Kansas, where I, boy lepidopterist,
future nomad of the lost countries of imagination,
felt the hand on my wrist, the Black Sea of not forgetting.

Mrs. Tate, for instance, stunning the dusty air
with *casta diva* in the tar-paper shack's backyard
littered with lenses, trays, tripods, the rusted remains
of camera equipment strewn with drunken care
by her husband, artist and disciple of Lewis Hine,
now failed in his craft but applauding his wife's
shrill arias Friday nights when the deaf town died
to rise again on Sunday and a boy listened across
the road to what might be, he thought, happiness.

The nameless one, garbage picker, hag of the alleys,
the town's bad dream scavenging trash cans
at 3 a.m. while I, sneaking from bed, edged closer
in the shadows, and she in her legendary madness
clawed through egg cartons, bottles, headless dolls.
Junk madonna in a high school formal, she cried
her lover's name, turning then with outspread hands,
reaching to hold my head against her hard breast,
sour smell of old crinoline, the terror of love.

And Miss Harp, bent over a cup of steaming tea,
sipping a novel fat as Falstaff, wheezing, thick-lensed,
sister of the holy order of spinster librarians,
cousin to the brothers Karamazov and Becky Sharp.
She called out my name, her piccolo voice doing
scales, and handed me an armload of new arrivals:
Dr. Zhivago, Kon-Tiki, A Boy's Guide to Aeronautics.
Her watery eyes bloomed, her quavering hand nudged
my shoulder: *Russia, adventure, the mystery of flight.*

Mazurkas drift down from the gazebo, troikas
clatter along the dark avenues of Yalta lined with
cypresses and firs. Behind a hedge of black thorn
we stroll the esplanade as a sexton tolls the bell
of some distant church. Mrs. Tate unfurls her
unnecessary parasol, and the librarian remarks
the harsh ocean air that fogs the street lamps.
A third woman takes my arm, humming lightly,
smiling, her porcelain hand calm upon my wrist.

Song

Gesang ist Dasein.

A small thing done well, the steel bit paring
the cut end of the collar, lifting delicate
blue spirals of iron slowly out of lamplight

into darkness until they broke and fell
into a pool of oil and water below.
A small thing done well, my father said

so often that I tired of hearing it and lost
myself in the shop's north end, an underworld
of welders who wore black masks and stared

through smoked glass where all was midnight
except the purest spark, the blue-white arc
of the clamp and rod. Hammers made dull tunes

hacking slag, and acetylene flames cast shadows
of men against the tin roof like great birds
trapped in diminishing circles of light.

Each day was like another. I stood beside him
and watched the lathe spin on, coils of iron
climbing into dusk, the file's drone, the rasp,

and finally the honing cloth with its small song
of things done well that I would carry into sleep
and dreams of men with wings of fire and steel.

Bert Fairchild, 1906-1990

At the Excavation of Liberal, Kansas

IN MEMORY OF WILLIAM STAFFORD

The whole town, with its daily minutiae,
was submerged by a . . . mix of ash,
pumice, and gases, from the volcano. . . .
Luncheon still waits on tables.
— Joseph Jay Dies, *Herculaneum*

The plains: the held breath of the earth.
Hysteria of noon, the shrill, metallic sun,
but at night, the wind's rasp and soughing, lunatic scrawls
of tree branches across a back-lit scrim of sky.

The town: necropolis, utopia of the dead.

Main street: their dwellings, shops, worn paths of daily commerce,
florid signatures of merchants—Firestone, Anthony's,
   Mode O'Day.
Throngs of citizens, now fallen, once driven by the urgencies
of trade and purchase.

The bronze plunder of brick streets
that shatter the day's last light.

CASEY'S RECREATION: its choir of long tables,
the exquisitely honed and painted balls. Imagine:
the tossing of the balls; the ancient tones of the gaudy instrument
named WURLITZER; amber bottles that, once restored,
   gleam in sunlight;
and the figures of young men, some of whom even in agony
still grip their slender wooden lances.

The ROBINSON HOTEL. I see the inhabitants rising each
    evening
in moonlight to sing from the windows
of their amazing loneliness, to call down to others, to invite them,
beckoning with their white arms and strange, splayed hands.

Automobiles. Ford, Chevrolet, Dodge. They only roll.
The artisan's weariness is evident everywhere.

MAIZELL'S COFFEE STOP: a ruin of aluminum and chrome
    handles,
their dull shine and muted curves. The names, HAMILTON BEACH,
FARMER BROTHERS, DIXIE, the embossed plaque reading
    ROTARIANS.
Lampshades like inverted flowers, counter chairs shy,
anonymous, still shaped by the press of thighs, the curve of spines.

Mirrors in every dwelling: a charm against loneliness?
The narcissism of a race whose portraits praise, always, the face?
A constant reprieve from forgetfulness (who am I, there I am)?

INDEPENDENT HARDWARE: the crescent wrench, the claw
    hammer,
the rope-and-pulley.

The huge white structure used for storing
and dispensing grain would have been visible for miles.
CO-OP. I see the populace in long lines waiting for their weekly
    portion
of wheat and oats, standing in the collective beauty
of rose petals: serried gatherings at the door of each bin,

the upturned faces, palms cupped, desire and fulfillment.
Then the long walk home in the cool of morning,
the heap of grain brilliant as coins on the kitchen floor.

a shirt, a glove, a shoe, a hat.

In BERRY'S FEEDSTORE behind the barrels and big cloth bags
is a box of calendars, illuminated with the same picture
of golden trees, a stream, an ancient water wheel.
Such common beauty was a daily reminder, of course,
of the hollowness of measurement,
the ephemeral lushness of the world in its flight toward oblivion,
the sterility of abstraction and calculation
and everything beyond the caught moment.
Those gilded leaves! Those groves!
Imagine the patrons walking up to discover the name of the day,
to mourn the beauty of its passing.

CHURCH OF THE NAZARENE, SACRED HEART, SOCIETY
  OF FRIENDS.

At the edge of town a tin building
with C&W MACHINE WORKS painted on its roof
is filled with lathes and other devices
perhaps involving crafts best performed in solitude.
The beautiful artifacts called tools litter the floor.
The fallen workers seem like soft machines, gray under ash.

Behind the building is the foreman's dwelling,
his truck with its burden of iron and steel resting outside.
Through the backdoor are the kitchen and its implements

with their odd shapes and wooden handles,
a clock in the shape of an exploding star, yellow chairs.
A photograph hangs on the wall: the foreman, his wife,
the boy between them, frowning.

(On the table lies a book
opened to a poem. Was it, I wonder, the boy's book?
Was the poem important to him? Did he carry it with him,
knowing that it was his life, his future?)

What I Heard Whispered at the Edge of Liberal, Kansas

Air waits for us
after we fall. It comes
perfectly together, just as a lake
does, in its every share giving
the fish paths as long
as they last. For us,
air contains all. After
we fall it waits. At the last
it is frantic with its hands
but cannot find us.
Was it a friend? Now,
too late, we think it was.

That's why we became grass.

—*William Stafford*

Thermoregulation in Winter Moths

How do the winter moths survive when other moths die?
What enables them to avoid freezing as they rest,
and what makes it possible for them to fly—and so
to seek food and mates—in the cold?

             —Bernd Heinrich, *Scientific American*

1. The Himalayas

The room lies there, immaculate, bone light
on white walls, shell-pink carpet, and pale, too,
are the wrists and hands of professors gathered
in the outer hall where behind darkness
and a mirror they can observe unseen.
They were told: high in the Himalayas
Buddhist monks thrive in sub-zero cold
far too harsh for human life. Suspended
in the deep grace of meditation, they raise
their body heat and do not freeze to death.
So five Tibetan monks have been flown
to Cambridge and the basement of Reed Hall.
They sit now with crossed legs and slight smiles,
and white sheets lap over their shoulders
like enfolded wings. The sheets are wet,
and drops of water trickle down the monks'
bare backs. The professors wait patiently
but with the widened eyes of fathers
watching new babies in hospital cribs.
Their aluminum clipboards rest gently
in their laps, their pens are poised,
and in a well-lit room in Cambridge
five Tibetan monks sit under heavy wet sheets
and steam begins to rise from their shoulders.

2. Burn Ward

My friend speaks haltingly, the syllables freezing
against the night air because the nurse's story
still possesses him, the ease with which she tended
patients so lost in pain, so mangled, scarred, and
abandoned in some arctic zone of uncharted suffering
that strangers stumbling onto the ward might
cry out, rushing back to a world where the very air
did not grieve flesh. *Empathy was impossible,*
he said. A kind of fog or frozen lake lay between her
and the patient, far away. Empathy was an insult,
to look into the eyes of the consumed and pretend,
I know. It must have been this lake, this vast
glacial plain that she would never cross, where
the patient waved in the blue-gray distance,
alone and trembling the way winter moths tremble
to warm themselves, while she stood, also alone
and freezing, on the other side, it must have been
this unbearable cold that made her drive straight home
one day, sit down cross-legged in the center of
an empty garage, pour the gasoline on like a balm,
and calmly strike a match like someone starting
a winter fire, or lost and searching in the frozen dark.

Kansas

Leaning against my car after changing the oil,
I hold my black hands out and stare into them
as if they were the faces of my children looking
at the winter moon and thinking of the snow
that will erase everything before they wake.

In the garage, my wife comes behind me
and slides her hands beneath my soiled shirt.
Pressing her face between my shoulder blades,
she mumbles something, and soon we are laughing,
wrestling like children among piles of old rags,

towels that unravel endlessly, torn sheets,
work shirts from twenty years ago when I stood
in the door of a machine shop, grease-blackened,
and Kansas lay before me blazing with new snow,
a future of flat land, white skies, and sunlight.

After making love, we lie on the abandoned
mattress and stare at our pale winter bodies
sprawling in the half-light. She touches her belly,
the scar of our last child, and the black prints
of my hands along her hips and thighs.

Keats

I knew him. He ran the lathe next to mine.
Perfectionist, a madman, even on overtime
Saturday night. Hum of the crowd floating
from the ball park, shouts, slamming doors
from the bar down the street, he would lean
into the lathe and make a little song
with the honing cloth, rubbing the edges,
smiling like a man asleep, dreaming.
A short guy, but fearless. At Margie's
he would take no lip, put the mechanic big
as a Buick through a stack of crates out back
and walked away with a broken thumb
but never said a word. Marge was a loud,
dirty girl with booze breath and bad manners.
He loved her. One night late I saw them in
the kitchen dancing something like a rhumba
to the radio, dishtowels wrapped around
their heads like swamis. Their laughter chimed
rich as brass rivets rolling down a tin roof.
But it was the work that kept him out of fights,
and I remember the red hair flaming
beneath the lamp, calipers measuring out
the last cut, his hands flicking iron burrs
like shooting stars through the shadows.
It was the iron, cut to a perfect fit, smooth
as bone china and gleaming under lamplight
that made him stand back, take out a smoke,
and sing. It was the dust that got him, his lungs
collapsed from breathing in a life of work.
Lying there, his hands are what I can't forget.

The Ascension of Ira Campbell

So there was Campbell rising in a scream
on the yellow travelling block that carried
five thousand feet of drill pipe in and out
of the hard summer earth that abideth ever,
paperback *Tractatus* sticking from his hip pocket.
Student and roughneck, Campbell dug his gloves
into the gray swag of metaphysics
and came up empty, but here on the wordless
and wind-flattened high plains he sang,
*Whereof one cannot speak, thereof one must
be silent.* He toiled, looting every
proposition for its true spirit, said
it was the end of language, the dark rustle
of the soul's wings that would haul the mind
beyond meaning. *It's all here, Fairchild,*
he screamed, waving the red book above his head,
the cables moaning, Campbell ascending
into the cloud-strewn facts of the sky,
blue or not blue, a sky amazingly itself.

The Dumka

His parents would sit alone together
on the blue divan in the small living room
listening to Dvorak's piano quintet.
They would sit there in their old age,
side by side, quite still, backs rigid, hands
in their laps, and look straight ahead
at the yellow light of the phonograph
that seemed as distant as a lamplit
window seen across the plains late at night.
They would sit quietly as something dense

and radiant swirled around them, something
like the dust storms of the thirties that began
by smearing the sky green with doom
but afterwards drenched the air with an amber
glow and then vanished, leaving profiles
of children on pillows and a pale gauze
over mantles and table tops. But it was
the memory of dust that encircled them now
and made them smile faintly and raise
or bow their heads as they spoke about

the farm in twilight with piano music
spiraling out across red roads and fields
of maize, bread lines in the city, women
and men lining main street like mannequins,
and then the war, the white frame rent house,
and the homecoming, the homecoming,
the homecoming, and afterwards, green lawns
and a new piano with its mahogany gleam
like pond ice at dawn, and now alone
in the house in the vanishing neighborhood,

the slow mornings of coffee and newspapers
and evenings of music and scattered bits
of talk like leaves suddenly fallen before
one notices the new season. And they would sit
there alone and soon he would reach across
and lift her hand as if it were the last unbroken
leaf and he would hold her hand in his hand
for a long time and they would look far off
into the music of their lives as they sat alone
together in the room in the house in Kansas.

A Model of Downtown Los Angeles, 1940

It's a bright, guilty world.
    —Orson Welles in *The Lady from Shanghai*

But there is no water.
    —T.S. Eliot, *The Waste Land*

The oldest Mercedes in California adorns
the crowded foyer of the L.A. County Museum
of Natural History, and babies shriek like bats
in the elevator that lowers my daughter
and me to the basement. There, among the faint,
intermingled drifts of ammonia and urine
from the men's room, phantom display lights
luring shadows over the inventions of Edison
and Bell, and dusty monuments to a century
of industrial progress, lies the mock-up L.A.,

whose perusal has been assigned to my daughter's
fourth-grade class in California history.
Fallen into ruin, its plexiglass sky yellowing
and covered with cracks, the fault lines of heaven,
it is soon to be hauled off with the duplicate
rhino horns and kachina dolls dulled with varnish.
Sarah circles the city, her face looming
large as a god's over buildings, across avenues
and boulevards from Vignes to Macy, then back
around to the borders of Beaudry and Eighth Street,

where in 1938 my father sat alone
in the Tiptop Diner and made tomato soup
from a free bowl of hot water and catsup.
Across the street was the office of the L.A. Times
where several upstanding Christian men had conspired
to steal the water from the Owens Valley.
Our farm became a scrap yard of rotted pears,
a bone yard, irrigation canals dried up
and turned to sage. A thousand lives in ruin
while L.A.'s San Fernando Valley rose

from desert into orange groves and, overnight,
made a fortune for the city fathers. One day
our hayrack caught fire and there was hell
in the air. On the roof, my father saw
in the distance a Hindu city with camels,
water buffalo, and four elephants: *Gunga Din*.
Water gone, vultures circling, Hollywood
was moving in. We followed Mulholland's
aqueduct south to L.A. and the cool dark
of the Pantages Theatre in blazing August

while my father hunted for cheap housing,
shacks with swamp boxes near Echo Park.
Each day he rode the classifieds until
the bars looked better, drank warm Pabst
at Mickey's Hideout where Franz Werfel
sang Verdi arias and told him stories
of Garbo, Brecht, Huxley, and Thomas Mann.
Later, he worked the rigs on Signal Hill
for a dollar a day, slinging the pipe tongs
and coming home smelling of oil and mud.

The days: morning light opening the streets
like a huge hand, then the bruised fist
of evening, that incredible pink and blue
bleeding into night, and the homeless
in Pershing Square claiming their benches again.
That summer he was shipped to Okinawa,
the Japanese trucked like crates of oranges
to Manzanar near Lone Pine in the Owens Valley,
and I wandered among the jacarandas
and birds of paradise at the Public Library

reading the *Communist Manifesto*
and plotting revenge. But I was a child.
Now I study Blake's *Songs* in rare editions
at Huntington's Museum and Botanical Gardens
and imagine the great patron and his pals
looking down on L.A. from the veranda
and sighing, *Bill Mulholland made this city*,
as the sun pales once more beneath a purple fist.
So, here is the Hall of Records, and Union Station
where my father, returned from the Pacific,

swore that we would head back north again.
Last night on television a man named Rodney King
showed how the city had progressed beyond
its primitive beginnings, how the open hand
of the law could touch a man in his very bones.
And there, staring back from the west end
of Spring Street, is my daughter learning her lessons
as she bends down for a closer look, pale blue eyes
descending slowly over the city, setting like
twin suns above the Department of Water and Power.

After the Storm

The professor's books lie scattered
over the brown lawns, fluttering like gulls,
a loose sobbing that goes on and on.
Shirts, tablecloths, curtains struggle against hedge and bush,
lifting, then yielding.

Oleanders ruffle the yellow brim
of the burnt sky dropped like a hat
during the night. Dogs paw through clutter.
Silence gathers in the streets thick as a chorus,
morning's bad opera.

The welder's wife has found the jonquils,
bright offerings given to the tool shed, its tin roof
peeled back, splayed like astonished hands.
A mangled hose winds among the garden tools,
rusted shovels, rakes, the dead weight of work.

Pages from the professor's books
litter the shed floor and drape the shelves,
and the welder's wife, sick now
with memory, picks them
like stunted flowers and begins to read

the gray notes, marginalia
of another life, written to his children:
Paul, can you detect, seeping through Spinoza's axioms
the unmistakable smell of human sweat,
of a good man

trying deperately to salvage
what is best in us? Or *Sarah, isn't Hobbes*
suggesting that civilization is rather like
a hand-painted mirror that a barbaric world
occasionally holds up to itself?

The pages fall from her hands.
The neighbor's hen is digging in the ruined garden,
the north sky smeared with rain.
Everywhere, the hands of the victims hold pages
from the professor's books

heavy as the mulberry leaves staining the driveways,
damp with the storm's last rage,
given finally to the wreckage,
the splintered lattice,
ripped shingles from the homes of the living.

The Children

*. . . genially, Magoo-like, when in the street he might
pat the heads of water hydrants and parking meters,
taking these to be the heads of children.*
    —Oliver Sacks, *The Man Who Mistook His Wife for a Hat*

More than children: frail, disheveled angels,
the awful weight of their wings shrugged off,
light feet again in love with the earth. They sing
some celestial liturgy too brittle for my ears
and guard the souls of commuters from the beasts
that would otherwise surely drive them into hell.
As they stand against the Plymouths of this world,
the clock of eternity is upon their foreheads
and a red arrow will point them homeward again.
But for now, humming their requiem to human memory,
they usher me toward the vanishing point.
That there should be such beautiful little ones!
symmetrically arranged like the found objects
in Cornell's boxes—a postcard from Paris,
a thimble, the King of Diamonds, a porcelain doll.
I follow them along the streets whose names
are only trees to me, past the toyshop remembered
and forgotten repeatedly. As in a dream,
my own home, vaguely familiar, drifts toward me
buoyed by the music of my past: the *Kinderscenen*,
or mazurkas to annoy my father and wake up the cats.
As the poet of children wrote, *the altering eye
alters all*, for I was a boy of vision,
and childhood was a scene from *The Magic Flute*.

Here is my wife, the green Homburg floating
across the veranda, to guide me up the steps
that seem suddenly like the backs of turtles
returning to the open sea. Here are my paintings
giving onto pools and glades that only I can know,
and my old Bösendorfer with its ancient brown tones.
The chords rise beneath my fingers, a seamless
harmony between the seer and the seen, the spirit's
body, the body's prayer.
Evening drops down.
I sing the *Dichterliebe*, and my wife accompanies.
Outside, the voices of children are heard in the rain,
Und Nebelbilder steigen/ Wohl aus der Erd hervor,
and misty images rise/ from the earth.

Little Boy

The sun lowers on our backyard in Kansas,
and I am looking up through the circling spokes
of a bicycle asking my father as mindlessly
as I would ask if he ever saw Dimaggio or Mantle
why we dropped the bomb on those two towns
in Japan, and his face goes all wooden, the eyes
freezing like rabbits in headlights, the palm
of his hand slowly tapping the arm of a lawnchair
that has appeared in family photographs
since 1945, the shadow of my mother thrown
across it, the green Packard in the background
which my father said he bought because after Saipan
and Tinian and Okinawa, "I felt like they owed it to me."
These were names I didn't know, islands distant
as planets, anonymous. Where is Saipan?
Where is Okinawa? Where is the Pacific?
Could you see the cloud in the air like the smoke
from Eugene Messenbaum's semi, that huge cloud
when he rolled it out on highway 54 last winter?
The hand is hammering the chair arm, beating it,
and I know it's all wrong as I move backward
on the garage floor and watch his eyes watching
the sun in its evening burial and the spreading
silver light and then darkness over the farms
and vast, flat fields which I will grow so tired of,
so weary of years later that I will leave, watching
then as I do now his eyes as they take in the falling rag
of the sun, a level stare, a gaze that asks nothing
and gives nothing, the sun burning itself to ashes
constantly, the orange maize blackening in drought
and waste, and he can do nothing and neither can I.

Two Photographs

Winter light,
a white frame house filling the background
as in a dream—the bare branches
of a cottonwood, a piece of sky.
In the foreground, my father
as a young man, and a car, a Packard.

His body drapes the body
of the car, back pressed against the door,
elbows rigid on the window's lower edge,
leg bent, polished Florsheim resting
on the running board.
He holds a cigarette with a particular grace

or perhaps feigned casualness,
smoke curling up along the right sideburn.
The hair was slicked back only
moments before, and the head is bowed
slightly as he gazes almost
shyly into the eye of the shutter.

Winter light. It rises from his white shirt
in the way of Hopper paintings,
the hard, floating light.
It is there, too, in the second photograph
where I lean against my car:
cigarette, sleeves twice-rolled

to where the forearm's lower muscle
just begins, the hair sleekly dark,
a thin wire of anxiety

disturbing the eyebrows. White house,
tree, sky, this odd, surrounding bareness
that is everything I want to leave,

and already I see the highway narrowing
to the vanishing point
past the GANO grain elevators
and Methodist church spires until Kansas
is only a sea of brown fields
diminishing in the rearview mirror.

The light in its long evolution toward
my father and his son:
the eye of the shutter opens,
two white shirts burn in a black box,
burn still under lamplight,
and a car approaches the horizon.

The Welder, Visited by the Angel of Mercy

Something strange is the soul on the earth.
—George Trakl

Spilled melons rotting on the highway's shoulder sweeten
the air, their bruised rinds silvering under the half-moon.
A blown tire makes the pickup list into the shoulder
like a swamped boat, and the trailer that was torn loose

has a twisted tongue and hitch that he has cut away,
trimmed, and wants to weld back on. Beyond lie fields
of short grass where cattle moan and drift like clouds, hunks
of dark looming behind barbed wire. The welder, crooning

along with a Patsy Cline tune from the truck's radio,
smokes his third joint, and a cracked bottle of Haig and Haig
glitters among the weeds, the rank and swollen melons.
Back at St. Benedict's they're studying Augustine now,

the great rake in his moment sobbing beneath the fig trees,
the child somewhere singing, take and read, take and read.
What they are not doing is fucking around in a ditch
on the road to El Paso ass-deep in mushmelons

and a lame pickup packed with books that are scattered now
from hell to breakfast. Jesus. Flipping the black mask up,
he reaches into the can for a fresh rod, clamps it,
then stares into the evening sky. Stars. The blackened moon.

The red dust of the city at night. Roy Garcia,
a man in a landscape, tries to weld his truck and his life
back together, but forgetting to drop the mask back down,
he touches rod to iron, and the arc's flash hammers

his eyes as he stumbles, blind, among the fruit of the earth.
The flame raging through his brain spreads its scorched wings
in a dazzle of embers, lowering the welder, the good student,
into his grass bed, where the world lies down to sleep

until it wakes once more into the dream of Being:
Roy and Maria at breakfast, white cups of black coffee,
fresh melons in blue bowls, the books in leather bindings
standing like silent children along the western wall.

The Death of a Small Town

It's rather like snow: in the beginning,
immaculate, brilliant, the trees shocked
into a crystalline awareness of something

remarkable, like them, but not of them,
perfectly formed and yet formless.
You want to walk up and down in it,

this bleak, maizeless field of innocence
with its black twigs and blue leaves.
You want to feel the silence crunching

beneath your houseshoes, but soon everyone
is wallowing in it, the trees no longer
bear sunlight, the sky has dragged down

its gray dream, and now it's no longer snow
but something else, not water or even
its dumb cousin, mud, but something used,

ordinary, dull. Then one morning at 4 a.m.
you go out seeking that one feeble remnant,
you are so lonely, and of course you find

its absence. An odd thing, to come upon
an absence, to come upon a death, to come upon
what is left when everything is gone.

The Art of the Lathe

Leonardo imagined the first one.
The next was a pole lathe with a drive cord,
illustrated in Plumier's *L'art de tourner en perfection*.
Then Ramsden, Vauconson, the great Maudslay,
his student Roberts, Fox, Clement, Whitworth.

The long line of machinists to my left
lean into their work, ungloved hands adjusting the calipers,
tapping the bit lightly with their fingertips.
Each man withdraws into his house of work:
the rough cut, shearing of iron by tempered steel,
blue-black threads lifting like locks of hair,
then breaking over bevel and ridge.
Oil and water splash over the whitening bit, hissing.
The lathe on night-shift, moonlight silvering the bed-ways.

The old man I apprenticed with, Roy Garcia,
in silk shirt, khakis, and Florsheims. Cautious,
almost delicate explanations and slow,
shapely hand movements. Craft by repetition.
Haig and Haig behind the tool chest.

In Diderot's *Encyclopaedia*, an engraving
of a small machine shop: forge and bellows in back,
in the foreground a mandrel lathe turned by a boy.
It is late afternoon, and the copper light leaking in
from the street side of the shop just catches
his elbow, calf, shoe. Taverns begin to crowd
with workmen curling over their tankards,
still hearing in the rattle of carriages over cobblestone
the steady tap of the treadle,
the gasp and heave of the bellows.

The boy leaves the shop, cringing into the light,
and digs the grime from his fingernails, blue
from bruises. Walking home, he hears a clavier—
Couperin, maybe, a Bach toccata—from a window overhead.
Music, he thinks, *the beautiful.*
Tavern doors open. Voices. Grab and hustle of the street.
Cart wheels. The small room of his life. The darkening sky.

I listen to the clunk-and-slide of the milling machine,
Maudsley's art of clarity and precision: sculpture of poppet,
saddle, jack screw, pawl, cone-pulley,
the fit and mesh of gears, tooth in groove like interlaced fingers.
I think of Mozart folding and unfolding his napkin
as the notes sound in his head. The new machinist sings
    Patsy Cline,
I Fall to Pieces. Sparrows bicker overhead.
Screed of the grinder, the bandsaw's groan and wail.

In his boredom the boy in Diderot
studies again through the shop's open door
the buttresses of Suger's cathedral
and imagines the young Leonardo in his apprenticeship
staring through the window at Brunelleschi's dome,
solid yet miraculous, a resurrected body, floating above the city.

Outside, a cowbird cries, flapping up from the pipe rack,
the ruffling of wings like a quilt flung over a bed.
Snow settles on the tops of cans, black rings in a white field.
The stock, cut clean, gleams under lamplight.
After work, I wade back through the silence of the shop:
the lathes shut down, inert, like enormous animals in hibernation,
red oil rags lying limp on the shoulders

of machines, dust motes still climbing shafts
of dawn light, hook and hoist chain lying desultory
as an old drunk collapsed outside a bar,
barn sparrows pecking on the shores of oil puddles—
emptiness, wholeness; a cave, a cathedral.

As morning light washes the walls of Florence,
the boy Leonardo mixes paints in Verrocchio's shop
and watches the new apprentice muddle
the simple task of the Madonna's shawl.
Leonardo whistles a *canzone* and imagines
a lathe: the spindle, bit, and treadle, the gleam of brass.

Notes

"The Dumka": Dumka is the name of the second movement of the piano quintet, Op. 81 in A major, mentioned in the poem.

"A Model of Downtown Los Angeles, 1940": Although the story of the Owens Valley/ Los Angeles aqueduct is generally well known (and debated) in California, it may be less known elsewhere other than through the film, *Chinatown*, which is not, obviously, a documentary but a drama loosely based on the incidents leading to the construction of the aqueduct. In 1905, encouraged by repeated headlines in the L.A. Times declaring a state of drought, citizens of Los Angeles voted for a bond issue to finance the building of an aqueduct from the Owens Valley 230 miles northeast of the city, a project of astonishing proportions successfully carried out by the brilliant, self-taught engineer, William Mulholland. But the aqueduct was brought not to Los Angeles but rather to the San Fernando Valley a few miles northwest of L.A., where a group known as the San Fernando Valley land syndicate--including the owner of the L.A. Times, Henry Huntington, Moses Sherman (a member of the L.A. water board), and other fabulously wealthy men--had purchased thousands of acres of cheap land that would now be worth tens of millions of dollars. Two years after construction was completed, the San Fernando Valley was annexed to Los Angeles (thus, Noah Cross's famous line in *Chinatown*, "Either you bring the water to L.A., or you bring L.A. to the water"). Over the years, the effect upon farmers in the Owens Valley was disastrous, but the economic benefit to L.A. was beyond measure; it would be fair to speculate that without the aqueduct L.A. today would be a small city about the size of Tulsa, Oklahoma. In my poem, the story is told from the point-of-view of a former resident (and victim) of the Owens Valley. Other references: *Gunga Din* (1939) was filmed in the Owens Valley; Franz Werfel, author of *Song of Bernadette* and friend of Kafka, was a part of the European emigre community in L.A. during the late thirties and forties, along with Mann and the others named here; Manzanar was a prison camp for Japanese U.S. citizens during World War II; the Rodney King beating, widely televised, culminated in the L.A. riots of 1992.

"The Children": In addition to the central neurological disorder described in the epigraph, several other character details of the persona are adopted from Sacks' book. "The altering eye alters all" is a line from William Blake.

"The Art of the Lathe": Ramsden, Vauconson, and the others named here were major contributors to the development of the lathe and other machine tools. See W. Steeds, *A History of Machine Tools 1700-1910* (Oxford: Clarendon Press, 1969).

Acknowledgments

I wish to thank the National Endowment for the Arts and the Californi Arts Council, with whose support many of these poems were written; th Sewanee Writers Conference; and the MacDowell Colony, where th manuscript of this book was prepared for publication. Grateful acknow ledgment is also made to the following publications for poems which orig inally appeared in them (although, in some cases, in different form).

American Literary Review: "Thermoregulation in Winter Moths"
Caliban: "A Model of Downtown Los Angeles, 1940"
Kansas Quarterly: "Little Boy," "Old Women"
Jacaranda Review: "Kansas"
Nimrod: "The Art of the Lathe"
Poetry: "Old Men Playing Basketball"
Prairie Schooner: "The Himalayas"
Quarterly Review of Literature 50th Anniversary Anthology: "The Ascension of Ira Campbell," "The Death of a Small Town," "Song"
Sewanee Review: "After the Storm," "The Book of Hours," "In the House of the Latin Professor"
Southern Poetry Review: "Body and Soul"
Southern Review: "All the People in Hopper's Paintings," "Speaking tl Names," "Beauty"
Threepenny Review: "The Invisible Man"
TriQuarterly: "The Machinist, Teaching His Daughter to Play the Piano," "Work"

"The Machinist, Teaching His Daughter to Play the Piano," "Speaking the Names," "Work," and "Kansas" were reprinted in *Quarterly Review of Literature,* vol. XXX, 1991.

"Little Boy" and "Old Women" received the Seaton Poetry Award from *Kansas Quarterly.*

"Body and Soul" received the Guy Owen Prize from *Southern Poet Review.*

The opening epigraph is from E. L. Doctorow's essay, "James Wi at Kenyon," in his *Jack London, Hemingway, and the Constitution* (Ne York: Random House, 1993), p. 194. Used by permission of Rando House.

About the Author

B. H. Fairchild was born in Houston, Texas and grew up there and in small towns in west Texas, Oklahoma, and Kansas. He attended the University of Kansas and the University of Tulsa and now lives with his wife and daughter in Claremont, California. His poetry has received many awards and prizes, including an NEA Fellowship in Poetry, a California Arts Grant, a Walter E. Dakin Fellowship to the Sewanee Writers Conference, a National Writer's Union First Prize, an AWP Anniversary Award, and the 1996 Capricorn and 1997 Beatrice Hawley Awards for *The Art of the Lathe*. His poems have appeared in *Southern Review, Poetry, TriQuarterly, Hudson Review, Salmagundi, Sewanee Review,* and other journals and small magazines, and his poetry collections include *Local Knowledge, The System of Which the Body is One Part, Flight,* and *The Arrival of the Future.* He is also the author of *Such Holy Song,* a study of William Blake.

Recent Titles by Alice James Books

The Way Out, Lisa Sewell
Generation, Sharon Kraus
Middle Kingdom, Adrienne Su
Journey Fruit, Kinereth Gensler
We Live in Bodies, Ellen Doré Watson
Heavy Grace, Robert Cording
Proofreading the Histories, Nora Mitchell
We Have Gone to the Beach, Cynthia Huntington
The Wanderer King, Theodore Deppe
Girl Hurt, E. J. Miller Laino
The Moon Reflected Fire, Doug Anderson
Vox Angelica, Timothy Liu
Call and Response, Forrest Hamer
Ghost Letters, Richard McCann
Upside Down in the Dark, Carol Potter
Where Divinity Begins, Deborah DiNicola
The Wild Field, Rita Gabis

ALICE JAMES BOOKS has been publishing books since 1973. One of the few presses in the country that is run collectively, the cooperative selects manuscripts for publication through competitions. New authors become active members of the press, participating in editorial and production activities. The press, which places an emphasis on publishing women poets, was named for Alice James, sister of William and Henry, whose gift for writing was ignored and whose fine journal did not appear until after her death.